THANK YOU FOR CHOOSING US!
WE HOPE YOU ENJOY THIS COLORING BOOK.

THIS BOOK BELONGS TO:

_____

_____

2022 - ALL RIGHTS RESERVED

COLOR TEST PAGE

DON'T MAKE ME USE MY TEACHER VOICE

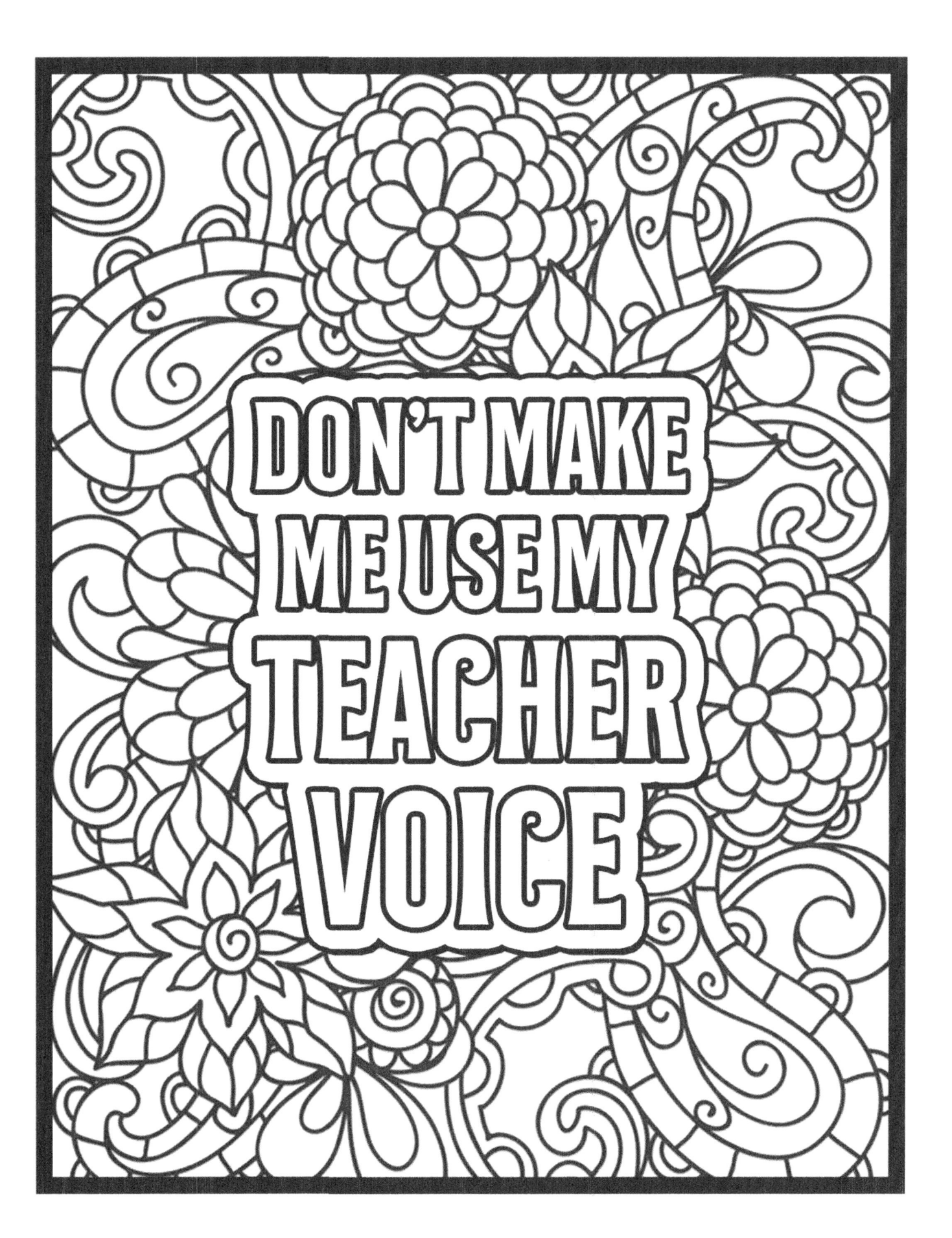

THIS TEACHER IS OFF DUTY

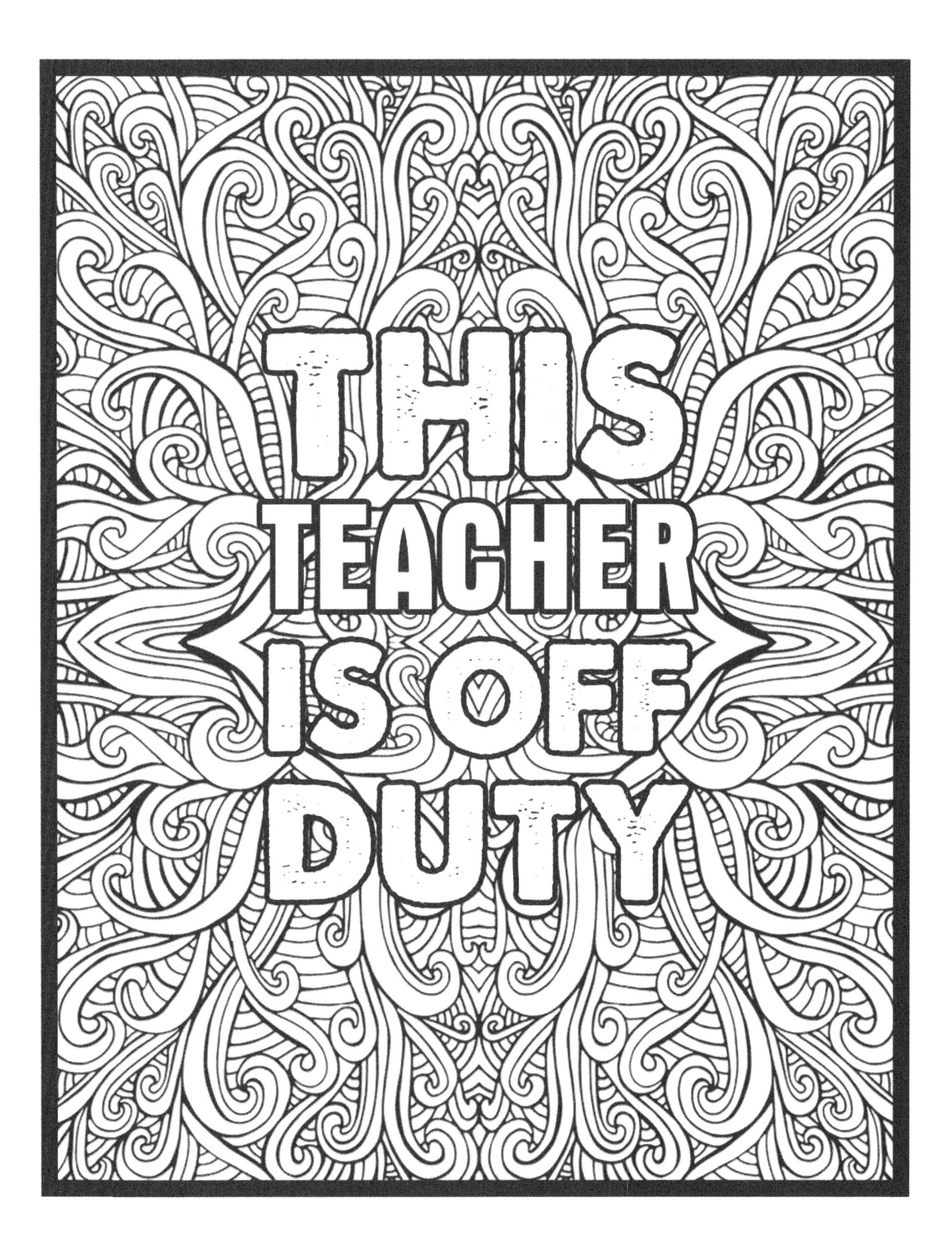

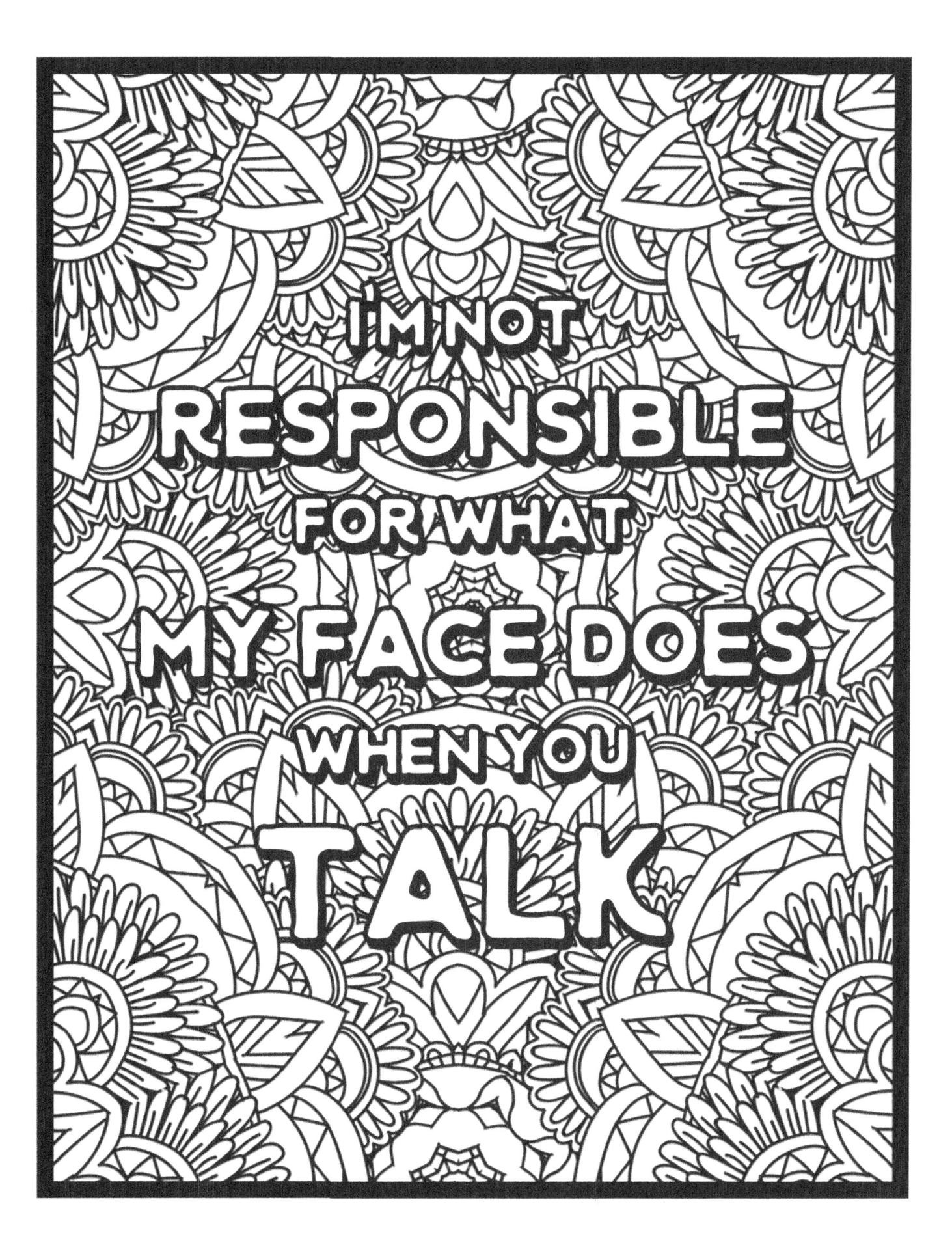

I'M NOT RESPONSIBLE FOR WHAT MY FACE DOES WHEN YOU TALK

World's Okayest Teacher

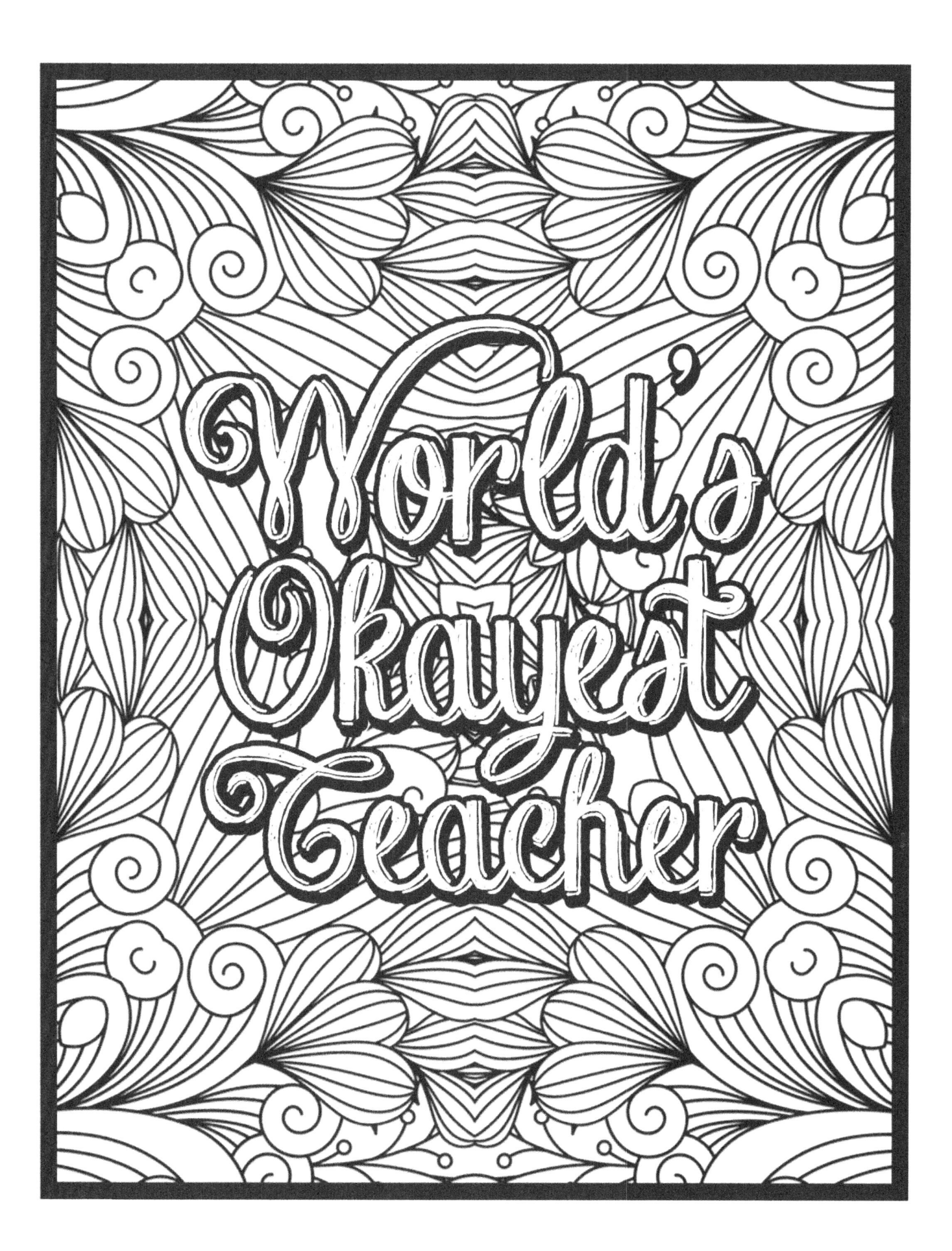

99% BADASS
01% TEACHER

Make Today Magical

SOME PEOPLE JUST NEED A HIGH-FIVE (IN THE FACE)

KEEP CALM AND LEAVE IT TO THE TEACHER

FRIDAY. MY 2ND FAVORITE F WORD.

SORRY I'M DONE HELPING ASSHOLES TODAY

TEACHER LLAMA AIN'T GOT TIME FOR YOUR DRAMA

I'M A TEACHER WHAT'S YOUR SUPER POWER?

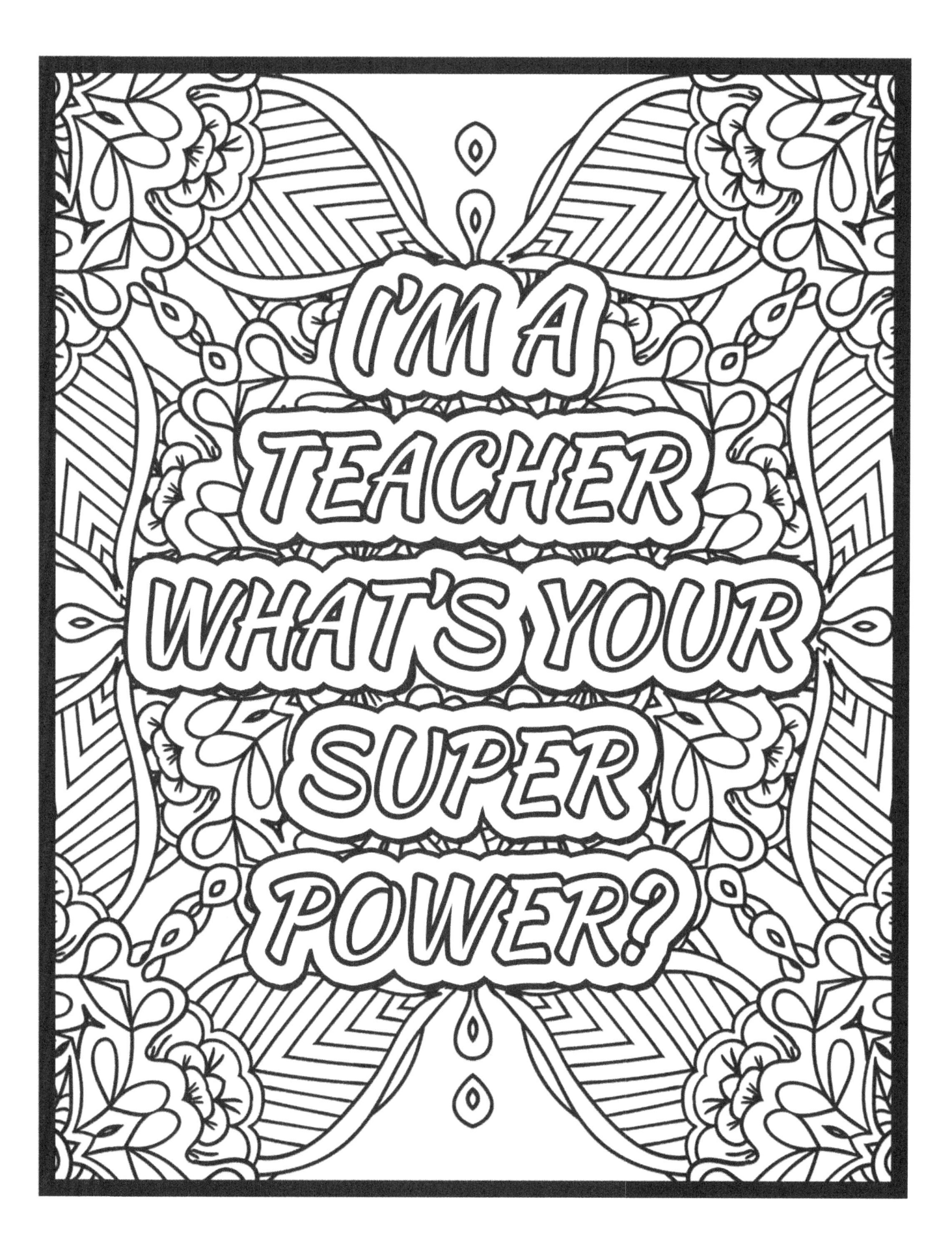

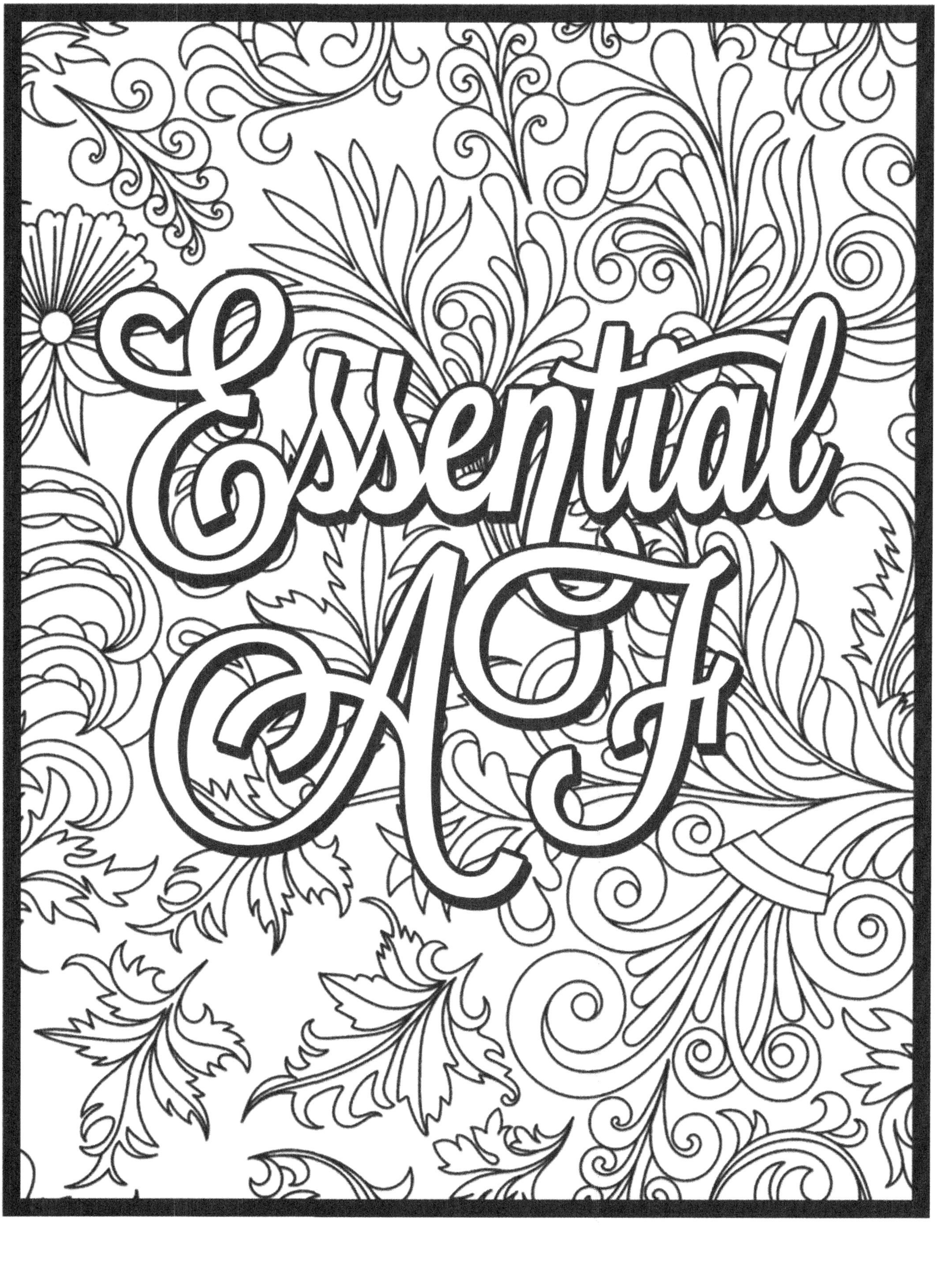
Essential
AF

INSTANT TEACHER JUST ADD COFFEE

Work?! I only need my Paychecks.

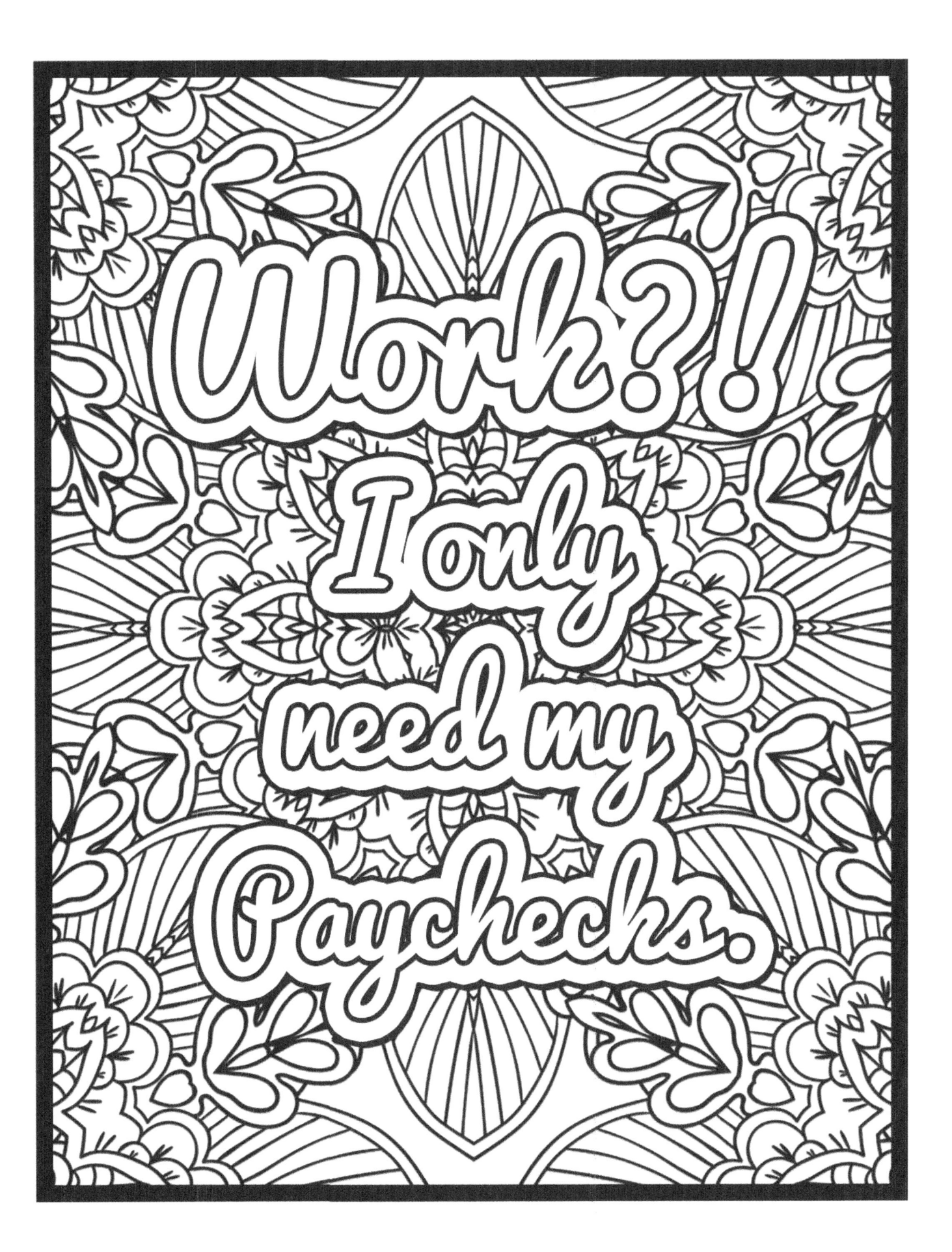

Best Teacher Ever

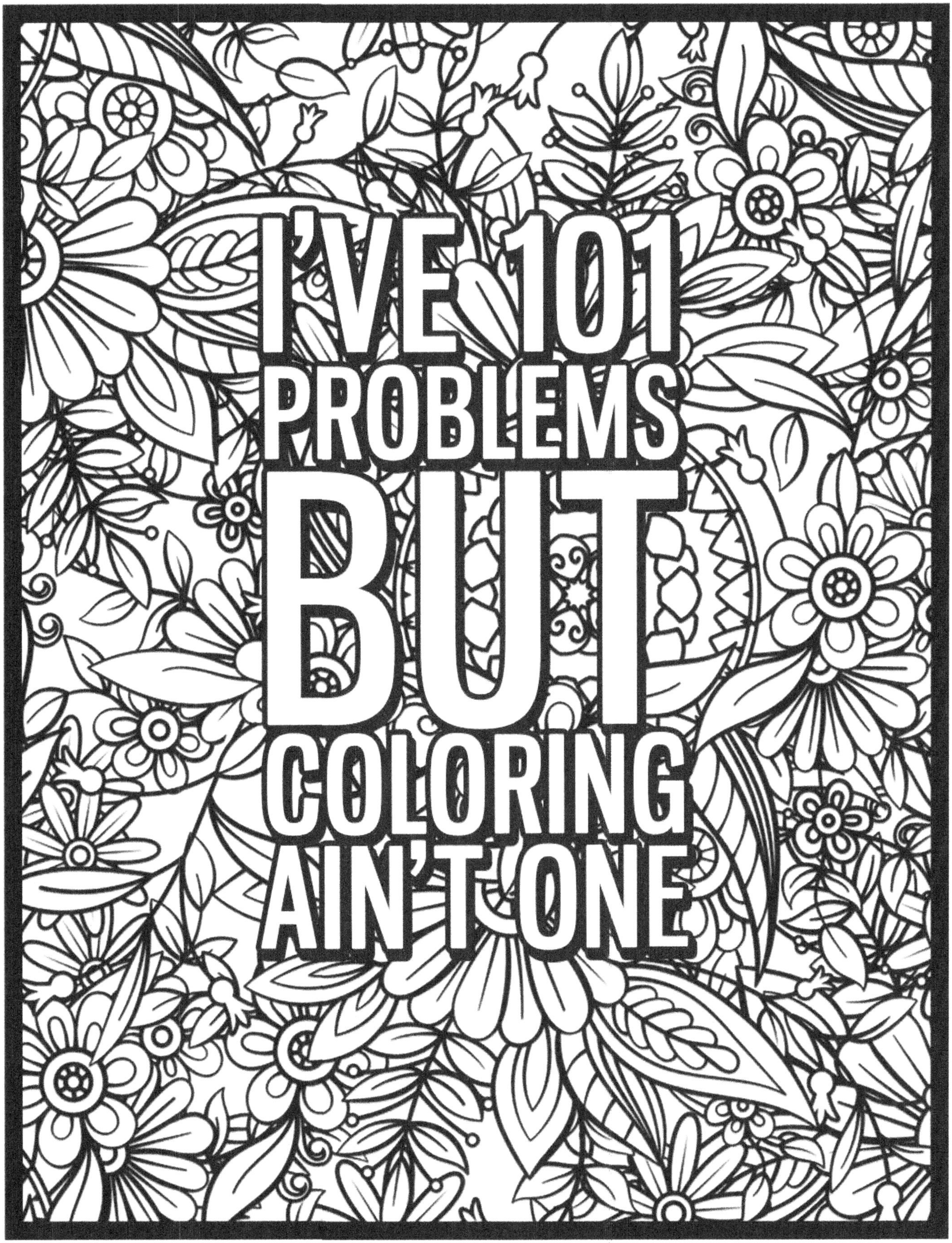
I'VE 101
PROBLEMS
BUT
COLORING
AIN'T ONE

I can't fix Stupid But I can Fix what Stupid Does

I'm a Nice Person Just Don't Push my Bitch Button!

It's a Teacher Thing You'd not Understand

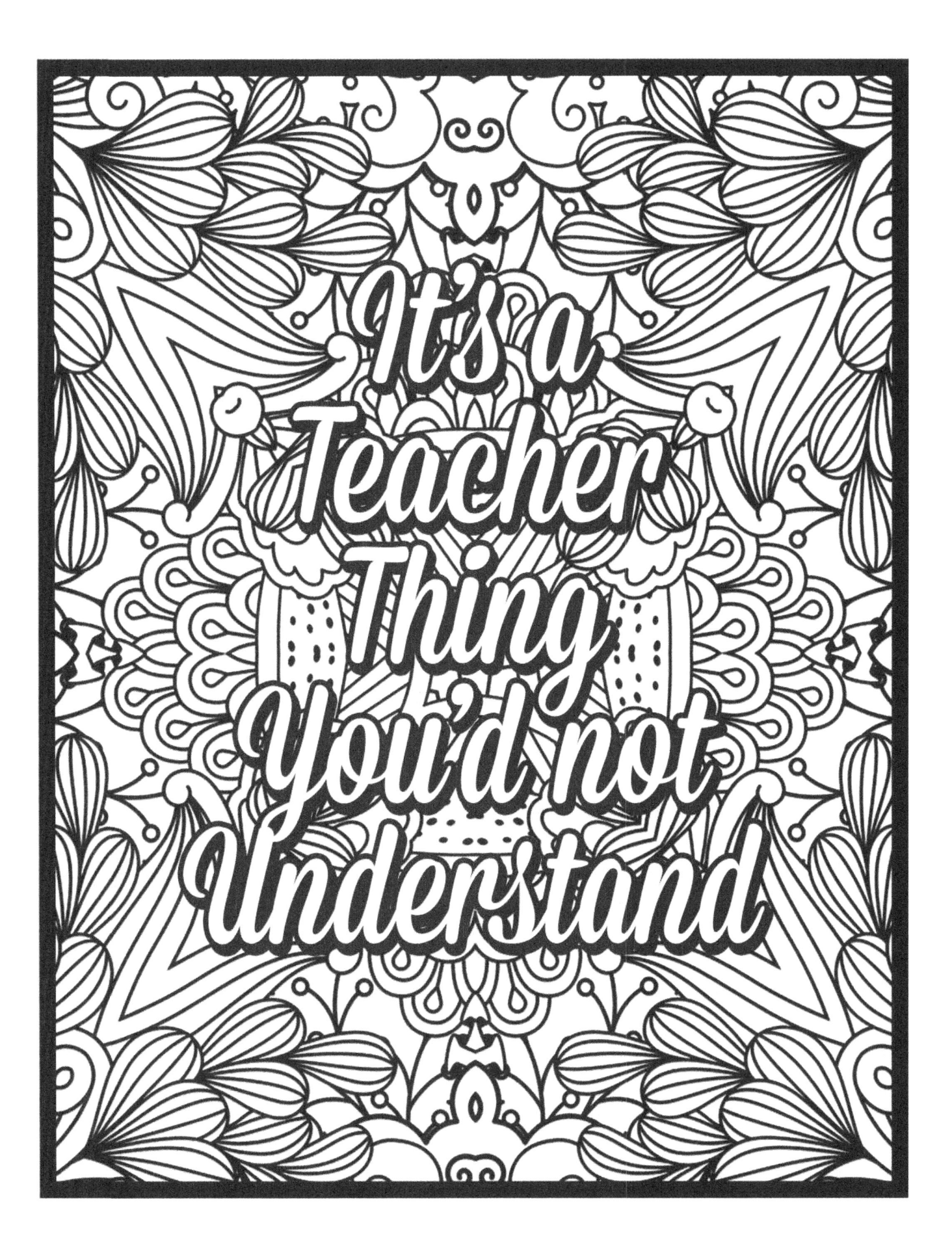